WALLS & WINDOWS - BARS & BRIDGES

YORK'S VISIBLE HISTORY

G A RHODES

First Published in 1993 by
Templar Publishing Marston Road
Tockwith Nr York YO5 8PR

© G A Rhodes 1993

ISBN 0 9521015 1 3

York's Visible History

British Library Catalogueing-In-Publication Data

A Catalogue Record for this book is available from The British Library

All rights reserved. No part of this book may be reproduced, stored in a retrieval system, or transmitted in any form or by whatever means, without prior permission of the publishers.

WALLS & WINDOWS - BARS & BRIDGES

YORK'S VISIBLE HISTORY.

THIS BOOK WOULD NOT HAVE BEEN POSSIBLE WITHOUT THE HELP OF THE FOLLOWING YORK COMPANIES

**DUNCAN GREAVES ASSOCIATES: ITSOKAYCO PRINTING:
KL PHOTOGRAPHIC LABORATORIES:
REPROTECH STUDIOS:
DAVID NEWTON & CO CERTIFIED ACCOUNTANTS:
TYPEWISE**

FOREWORD BY LORD FEVERSHAM, DUNCOMBE PARK, HELMSLEY, YORK

Our historic cities are becoming submerged under waves of signposts and bill-boards which threaten to obscure the very objects which they seek to locate and advertise.

Graham Rhodes wades into this sea of junk with the purpose of documenting the history of York through the eye of his camera, giving us a welcome opportunity to focus on the real progress of this great city through the ages.

Feversham

Vi . Viii . MCMIXCii

INTRODUCTION

I am delighted to be associated with this new book on the history of York. For the visitor and resident alike it should prove the ideal launching pad to discover the history of York as it has survived to the present day.

York is a living, thriving City which has learnt to adapt over the years to become what it is today. Its residents are proud of it and proud to be part of it but it is vital that the City does not become a museum; it must continue to adapt and change to meet the challenge of life in the 20th century while continuing to preserve the past.

The City has not always managed to get it right and I am sure that with hindsight there are many things that would be done differently now. But the wealth of buildings shown in this book demonstrates that it is possible to combine conservation with progress.

This is just the tip of the iceberg as far as the architectural wealth of the City is concerned. Enjoy the book for what it is but also use it as a stepping stone to discover more of what the beautiful city of York has to offer.

ANN REID
LORD MAYOR 1993-94

INTRODUCTION

It was King George VI who stated "The history of York is the history of England". Throughout this book I have attempted to photograph the remains of this history as it can still be found in the streets of York today. No photograph was taken from any spot where an entrance fee had to be paid. That's the nice thing about York's history - it's free, if you know where to look.

Today The City of York is a vibrant place, not just a living museum to be visited by tourists. It is populated by families and people who live and work in the City, and who, like their forebears, call York their home. Throughout this book, amongst the many tourists, these people can be seen going about their daily lives. I would like to dedicate this book to all these York people, and their families before them.

I would also like to thank Duncan Greaves, Dennis Kaye and Jonathan Cainer without whose help and generosity this book would have been impossible. Angela for proof reading, Elspeth Fraser-Darling and Andi Lee for their assistance.

G. A. Rhodes June 1993.

ALQUIN

Alquin the Anglo-Saxon scholar (c. 732-804) described York as "high-walled and towered" ...... "a merchant town of land and sea" . ..... "a haven for the ships from distant ports" ...... "watered by the fish-rich Ouse" ..... "a lovely dwelling place" ...... "whose health and richness will fill it full of men."

His description can still be used to describe the city today.

ROMAN YORK

Roman York was born around AD 71 when 6,000 men of the 9th Legion marched from Lincoln to invade the tribal lands of the Celtic Brigantes. To fight this campaign their commander, Quintus Petillus Cerialis, established a military base at a place known to the Celts as "Eburacon" - the Romans renamed the settlement "Eboracum".

In AD 108 Cerialis's original wooden fortress was replaced by one built from stone.

This new, rectangular fortress occupied a site of over 50 acres and eventually became the centre of a large walled and gated Roman city.

York was an important Roman city for over 340 years. It was granted the highest distinction that the Romans could be bestow, the title of Colonia.

It was here that Emperor Septimus Severus died and where, in AD 306, Constantine the Great was proclaimed Emperor of the Roman Empire.

The Roman Column

This Roman Column, discovered beneath York Minster, was once part of the headquarters building. It stands 30ft tall and has been re-erected opposite the Minster South Door.

The Roman Baths

In the basement of "The Roman Bath Inn", St Sampson's Square, are the preserved remains of a Roman Bath House. The original hot room can be seen through a glass panel in the lounge bar.

The Multangular Tower

This tower originally formed the western corner of the Roman fortress, and is one of the finest surviving examples of Roman masonry in Britain. Despite the upper part being a thirteenth century addition, the lower portion of the building is all fourth century.

ANGLIAN YORK.

Long before the Romans withdrew from Britain the city had become home to the Anglo-Saxons. These peoples had been invited to settle inside the city by the Romans and acted on their behalf as mercenaries, helping to defend the town from attacks by Picts and other tribal Britons.

After the Romans withdrawal (AD 410) the Anglo-Saxons took control of the city, renamed as Eoforwic, which eventually became the main royal and ecclesiastical centre of the Kingdom of Northumbria.

The church of St Mary's Bishophill Junior dates back to this period and has a tower that retains typical Saxon windows and herringbone masonry.

The Anglian Tower.

This building, tucked away behind the city library, dates from a period between AD 600 - 700, and is the bottom storey of a tower originally built by the Anglo Saxons to breach a hole in the Roman Wall. It was excavated in 1969 and is the only one of its type to be found in the country.

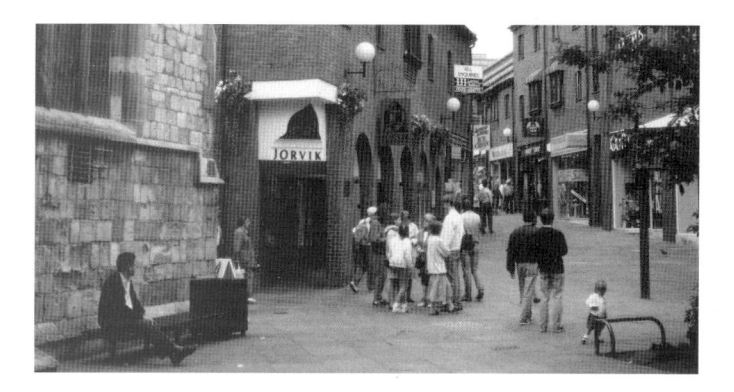

VIKING YORK.

The first Viking raids on the English coastline began at the end of the 8th century. Eventually the Viking objectives changed from harassment to settlement. In AD 865 a large Viking force known as the Great Army landed at East Anglia, and in the following year marched north and captured York.

The main Viking army travelled south to fight King Alfred, but a Viking named Halfdan led part of the army back to York and established a town, known as Jorvik, as the capital of a Viking kingdom.

This kingdom survived for 80 years until its last king, the Norwegian Eric Bloodaxe, was chased out of York by the English King Eadred in 954. However, the Northumbrians and the Vikings had intermixed so much that the Viking character of the town remained until the Norman Conquest.

The world famous "Coppergate Dig", begun in 1976, revealed the remains of Viking York. Over a five year period archaeologists uncovered the remains of houses and workshops that contained many utensils, tools, shoes and jewellery.

Built on the site of this dig, as an integral part of the Coppergate Centre, The Jorvik Viking Centre is a unique museum which incorporates original timbers and artefacts within a reconstruction of a Viking Street.

NORMAN YORK

The victory of William the Conqueror in 1066 brought an end to the Viking Kingdom. York was quickly captured and in 1068 William built the first of his wooden castles in the town. A second was completed in the following year and together these Norman castles formed two major defences on either side of the River Ouse.

In 1069 the people of York rebelled, and in an attempt to clear their besieged castle, the Normans set fire to the surrounding buildings. This fire spread to the town and engulfed most of Viking York. In response to this uprising William and his army travelled North and "laid to waste the shire and all that was in it."

The Norman House

Just off Stonegate, through a door and down one of York's many snickleways, are the restored remains of a 12th century Norman House. Its two remaining walls surround a small courtyard and show the existence of a two-storey building. Evidence suggests that the building was constructed around 1180, making it the city's oldest remaining dwelling.

William's Castles

The sites of the two wooden Norman "Motte and Bailey" castles still remain. At Baile Hill only the grass mound or "Motte" remains. The other castle, rebuilt with stone in the 13th century, is now known as Clifford's Tower.

St Mary's Abbey

St Mary's Abbey

Founded in 1088, the remains of St Mary's Abbey, once the richest Benedictine Abbey in the North, stand in York's Museum gardens. The original Norman Abbey was destroyed by fire in 1137, and the present building dates from its rebuilding which commenced in 1271. The Abbey was dissolved in 1539 and partly demolished to provide building stone for many local buildings.

St Leonard's Hospital

These remains are the surviving corner of what was once the infirmary of the largest hospital in Northern England. Erected in the time of King Stephen, it held over 150 workers and 300 patients and was a rich, charitable institution. It distributed alms at its gate and every Sunday provided a dinner to prisoners held in York Castle.

York Minster

The official name of this building is "The Cathedral and Metropolitical Church of St Peter in York", but to residents and tourists alike it is simply known as "The Minster".

Since the beginning of York's history the site has always been one of major importance. It housed the Roman Principia, the military fortress. In AD 627 the site was chosen by King Edwin of Northumbria on which to build a small wooden church for his own baptism.

After Edwin's death the original wooden church was rebuilt in stone, by St Wilfred in about AD 670, only to be destroyed by fire when William the Conqueror laid waste to the North. William wanted the church to be rebuilt and employed Archbishop Thomas of Bayeux to undertake the task.

His building was enlarged by Archbishop Roger Pont L'Eveque between 1154 and 1181. The building process continued when Archbishop Walter De Grey envisaged the creation of a vast Cathedral and in 1227 he began a building programme, one that would take the next 250 years to complete.

Today York Minster is one of the finest surviving examples of English Gothic architecture and is the largest Gothic cathedral in Northern Europe.

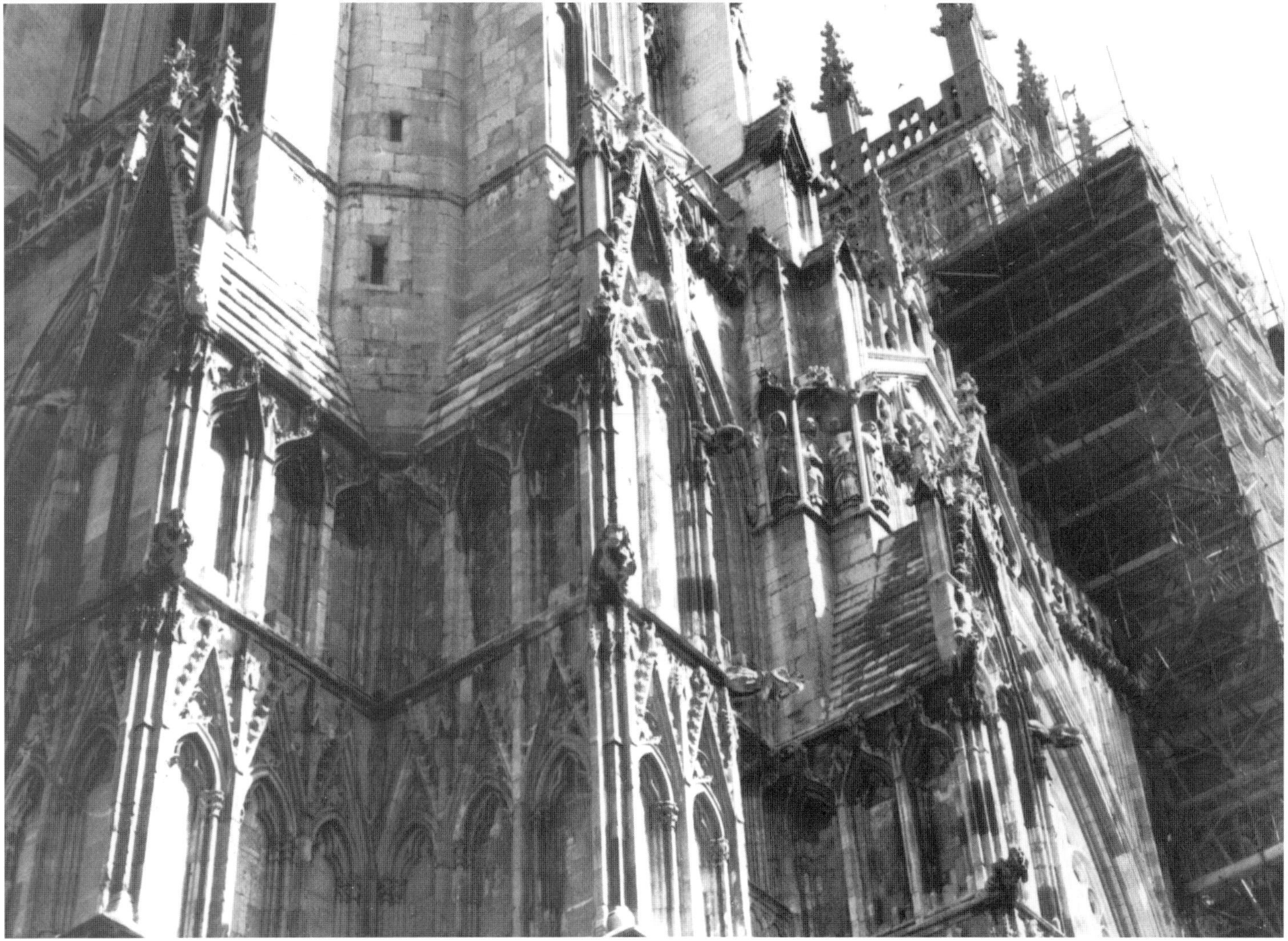

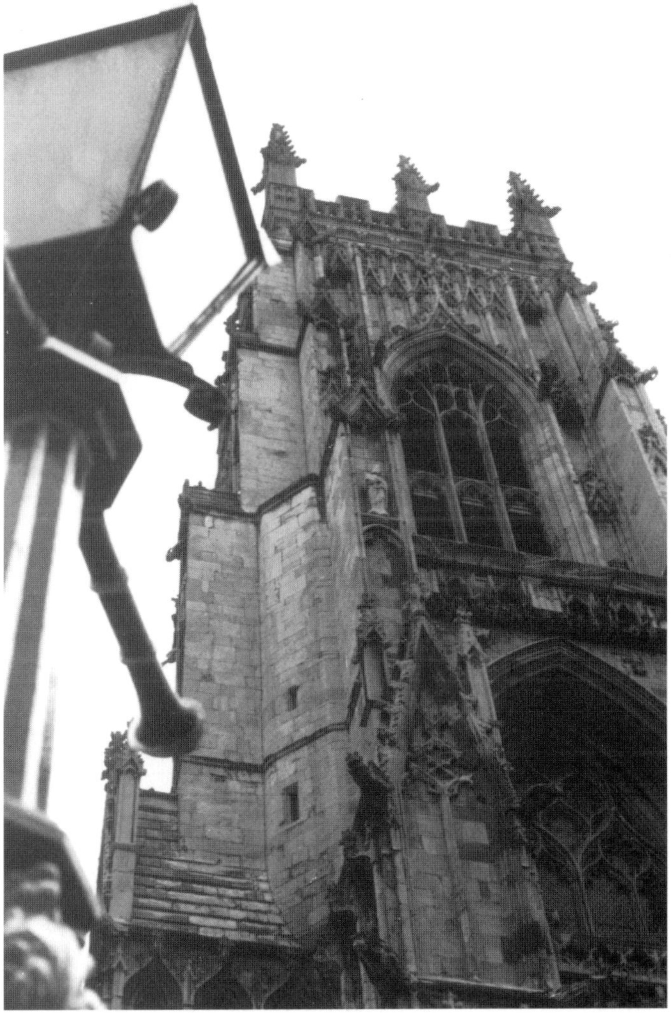

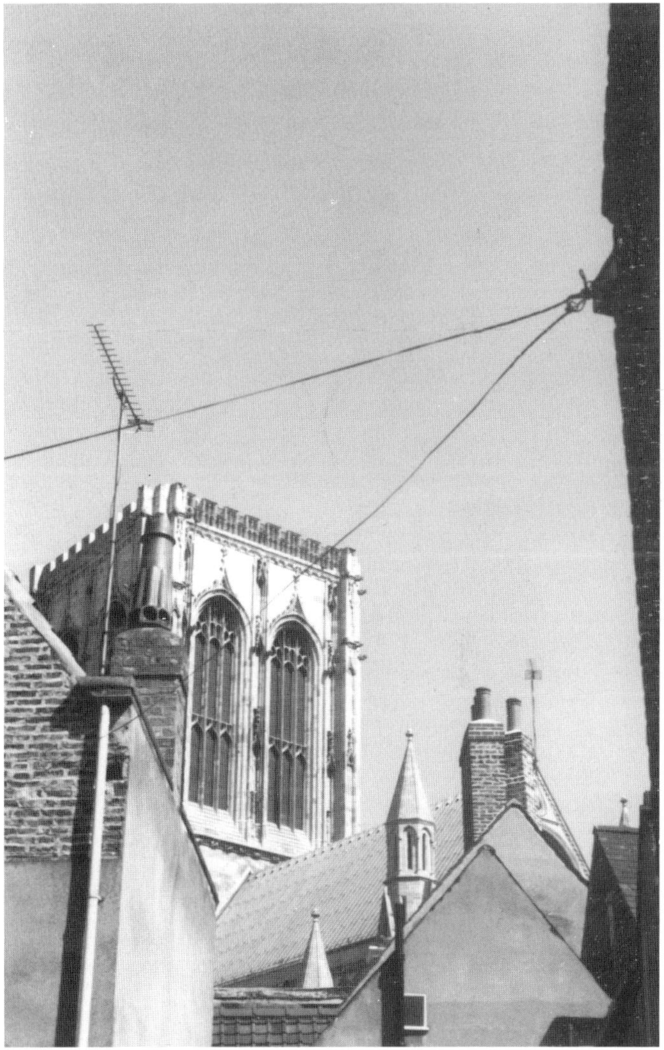

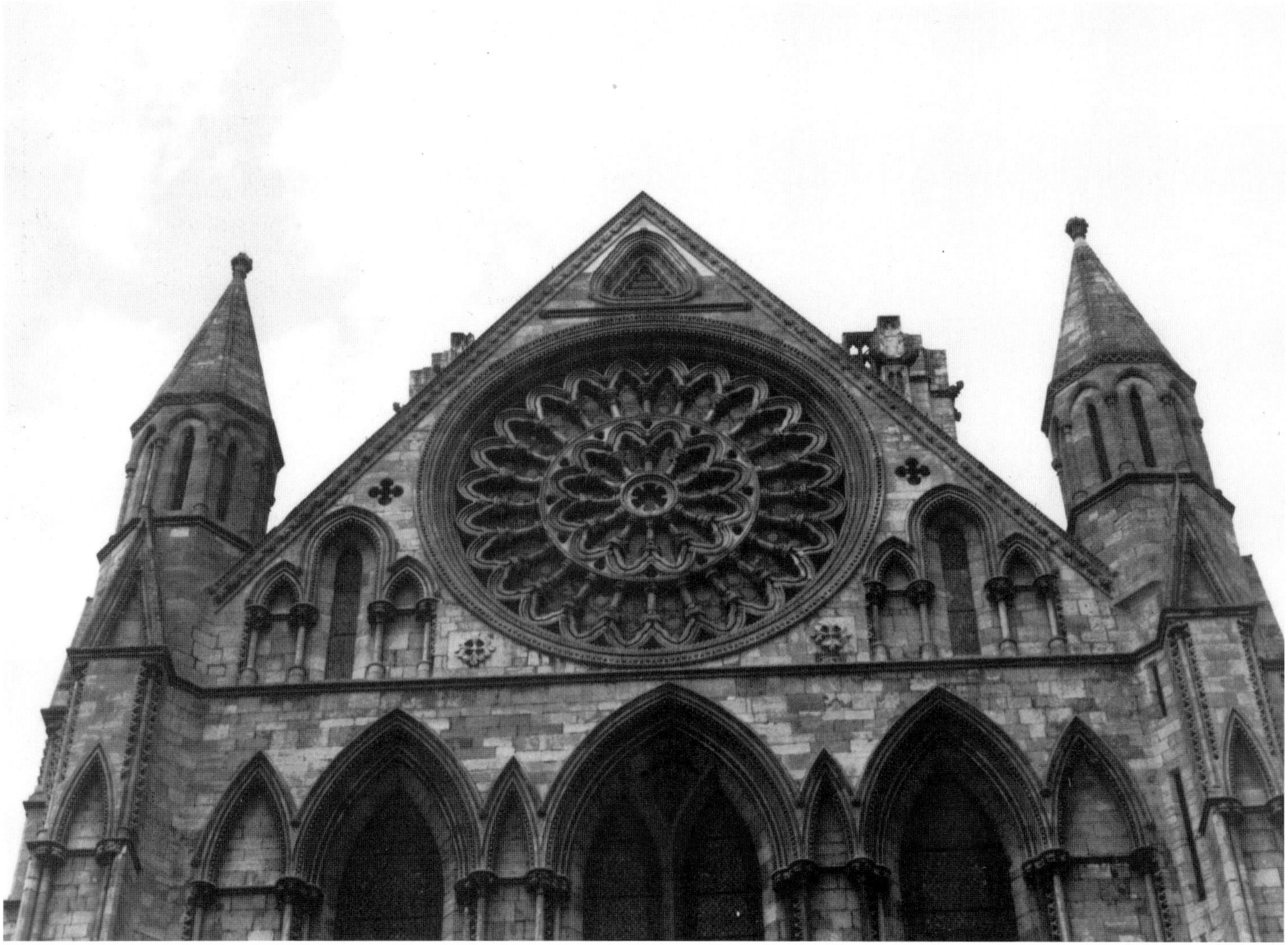

MEDIEVAL YORK

In the 250 years that it took to build York Minster the town also saw the development of its Walls and Bars, The Guildhall, the merchants' halls and the many streets that make today's York one of the finest medieval towns in Britain.

The City prospered, both as a port and a centre for trade. It became the northern capital of England and witnessed the arrival of many Kings and Queens. Henry I granted the city its first royal charter and in 1160 Henry II held his parliament in the town. The Minster saw the marriage of Henry III's sister and daughter and in 1328 the marriage of Edward III.

Richard III was fond of York and presented The City with its first Sword of State.

St Martin-Le-Grand, Coney Street.

Churches

As well as four monasteries, a nunnery, and several other religious houses, most of York's 40 or so medieval churches had been founded by the year 1250. Many of these Norman churches still survive though few retain their original Norman features.

St Cuthbert's, Peasholme Green

St Mary's, Castlegate

All Saint's, North Street

All Saint's, Pavement

26

St Olave's, Marygate

Holy Trinity, Micklegate

St Margaret's, Walmgate

St Deny's, St Deny's Road

St Martin-Cum-Gregory, Micklegate

Holy Trinity, Goodramgate

St Saviour's, St Saviourgate

St Helen's Church, St Helen's Square

The Merchant Adventurers' Hall

This building, virtually unchanged since it was built in 1357, originally housed a religious institution, "The Guild of Our Lord and the Blessed Virgin". However it eventually became the home of the Merchant Adventures' Company of the City of York.

This guild embraced all aspects of the woollen trade, and became one of the most powerful guilds in the City, dealing with the import and export of goods to and from York.

St William's College

The present half timbered building was erected between 1465-67 and was originally used to house the Chantry Priests of the Minster, but after the dissolution it became the home of private families. When Charles I moved his court to York the building was used to house the royal print works, but by the 18th century it had once again reverted to being used as tenements.

St William's College

The Walls and Bars

In 1250 the City Fathers set about the task of rebuilding York's ancient city walls. The resulting wall follows the line of its Roman predecessor, and stretches for almost three miles around the city. In addition to its four great entrances, Micklegate, Bootham, Walmgate, and Monk Bar, the City Wall contains many interesting smaller towers and entrances.

Over the centuries, as the town grew, the wall has seen many changes. Many alterations have been undertaken and new entrances created, allowing both railways and roads to pass through.

However the Corporation of York must be held responsible for the wholesale destruction wrought on the Bars in the early 1800's.

This short sighted Corporation not only promoted the idea of demolishing the walls and Bootham Bar, but also Clifford's Tower.

However, after a long and heated debate which saw leading citizens led by the eminent York painter William Etty unite against the Corporation, public pressure eventually won. In 1860 the walls were saved. Unfortunately it was too late for some small stretches of wall, a number of postern towers, and all the Bars' barbicans, with the exception of the one at Walmgate Bar, which had already been destroyed.

Micklegate Bar

35

Fishergate Postern Tower

North Street Postern Tower

Red Tower

Foss Islands Road

Foss Islands Road

Walmgate Bar

Walmgate Bar

Monk Bar

40

Fishergate Bar

Gillygate

Lord Mayor's Walk

Foss Islands Road

Bootham Bar

42

Victoria Bar

Micklegate Bar

Bootham Bar

43

The Shambles

The Shambles is possibly the best known medieval street in Britain. Originally it was a street of butchers, its name deriving from "Fleshshammels" or flesh benches, where meat was hung and displayed.

In medieval times the street would be filled with offal and other garbage which, coupled with poor sanitation and overcrowding, proved to be the source of the many plagues that haunted York between 12th & 17th Centuries.

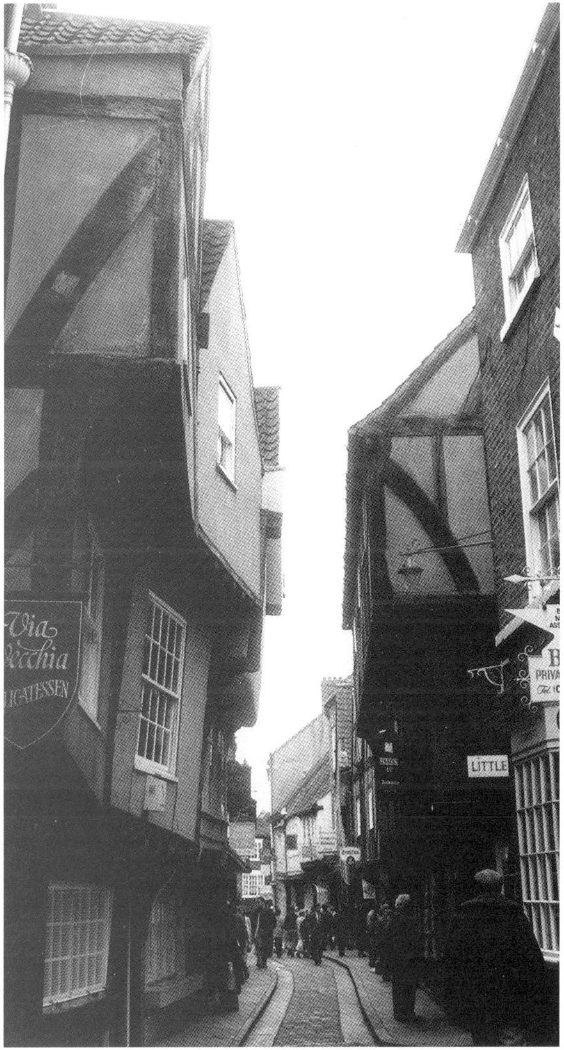
LITTLE

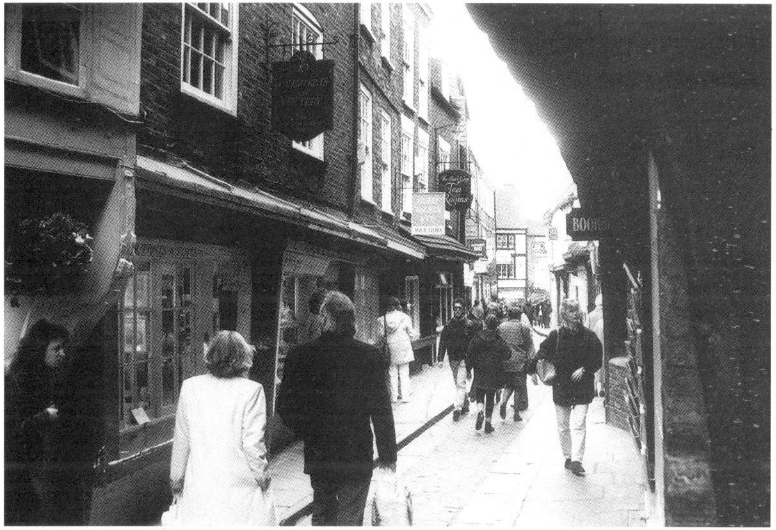

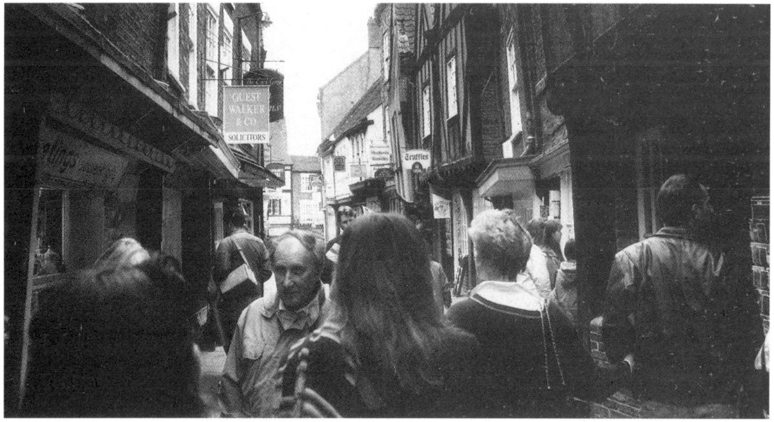
GUEST
WALKER
& CO
SOLICITORS
Truffles

Lady Row, Goodramgate

Built in 1316, this row of buildings comprises the oldest surviving cottages in York. Standing two storeys high and one room deep, they are England's earliest examples of jettied ranges - buildings where the upper floor overhangs the lower one.

The Guildhall

The Guildhall was built between 1447-59 to house the city's government after the original council chamber was moved from Ouse Bridge.

The original 15th century building was gutted during the York blitz in 1942. The present building is an exact replica and was opened by Queen Elizabeth The Queen Mother in 1960.

Stonegate

Stonegate has its origins in Roman times, and is York's most elegant medieval street. During Medieval times it was a street of booksellers, and in 1500 was the site of the earliest known York press. All of the original medieval buildings now have either Georgian, Regency or Victorian facades.

Stonegate was the birthplace of Guy Fawkes in 1570. Laurence Sterne (author of "Tristram Shandy") lodged in the street, and in 1682 number 35 became the site of Francis Hilyard's famous bookshop "The Sign of the Bible".

49

The Treasurer's House

The original Treasurer's House was built around 1100 and housed the Treasurer of York Minster. When this position was abolished during the Dissolution of the Monasteries, the house became a private dwelling.

It was re-built by one Thomas Young between 1628-1648, with further improvements being made around 1700 but by the 19th century the house was divided into three and eventually fell into decline. In 1897 it was purchased by Frank Green, a Yorkshire industrialist, who began a long restoration process. When he died in the 1930's he donated the house, together with its antique contents, to the National Trust.

51

King's Manor

Originally built in the late 1200's to house the Abbot of St Mary's, King's Manor was rebuilt in 1493. More building work was undertaken in 1560 when stone from the newly dissolved St Mary's Abbey was used. It was expanded again in the 1600's.

The house has strong royal connections. Henry VIII is reputed to have stayed there with Anne Boleyn and later with Catherine Howard. Both Charles I and Charles II stayed at the house, as did King James VI of Scotland on his way south to be crowned James I of England.

In its time the house has been a private dwelling, a girls' school and the home of The Yorkshire School for the Blind. Today it is part of the University of York.

GEORGIAN YORK

The Georgian era heralded into York a period of gentrification and elegance. The City became less important as a town of trade and commerce and instead became a centre of fashionable social life and culture.

Many of York's squalid, medieval half timbered houses, shops and streets, were replaced with fine new Georgian town houses and elegant public buildings.

New attractions were specially created for the amusement of the visiting gentry. York now offered a winter season of masques and balls, concerts, horse racing on the Knavesmire, and the spectacle of public executions at York Tyburn. Popular meeting places were the Theatre, The Assembly Rooms and the numerous cockpits and coffee houses that sprang up.

There was, however, another side to this elegance. Slums existed in areas such as Walmgate, Fossgate, Gillygate and Bishophill. In these areas unemployment, disease, poverty, and misery was the everyday existence for over half of the city's residents.

Micklegate

The Mount

Duncombe Place

Bootham

Micklegate

Bootham

55

Fairfax House, Castlegate

Fairfax House has been described as one of the finest 18th century town houses remaining in Britain. It was originally a much older building, but when Lord Fairfax bought the property in 1760 he employed the York architect John Carr to totally re build the interior.

The house was fully renovated by the York Civic Trust and was officially opened by The Duchess of Kent in 1984. Today the building contains a treasure house of Georgian art and furniture known as the Noel Terry Collection.

The Assembly Rooms

The Assembly Rooms were built in 1730 and represent one of Europe's earliest examples of an architectural style called Neo-Classical. In their heyday the Assembly Rooms saw great balls, assemblies and routs and soon they became the centre of fashionable York society.

York Theatre Royal

The need to extend the York season created the need for a theatre, and eventually one opened in a tennis court in what is now Minster Yard. The New Theatre first opened on its present site in 1744, and was granted its Royal licence in 1769. The theatre was substantially rebuilt with the Victorian gothic facade being completed in 1888. The new foyer was added in 1967 and built in the typical 1960's glass and concrete style.

The Knavesmire

The Knavesmire is the name of the large common pasture that contains both York racecourse and the site of the once infamous city gallows, York Tyburn.

York has a history of horse racing that dates back to 1530 when an annual race ran through the Forest of Galtres. In the August of 1714 the first Kings Cup was run at Clifton Ings, and in 1731 the racecourse moved to the Knavesmire. York architect John Carr established his reputation with the building of the first grandstand in 1755.

The York Prisons

The Debtors' Prison
The Debtors' Prison, built between 1701-05, was described by Defoe as being "the most stately and complete prison of any in the Kingdom".

The Assize Courts
The Assize Courts, built between 1773 and 1777, were designed by John Carr. The two court rooms, still in use today, have witnessed the trials of Dick Turpin, The Luddites and the Peterloo Rioters.

The Female Prison
The Female Prison was added in 1780 to alleviate overcrowding in the Debtors Prison, It was also designed by John Carr to complement the Assize Courts which stand opposite.

In the 19th Century another prison building was added and the entire area, including Clifford's Tower, was enclosed by a high wall. When the Female Prison closed in the 1930's the outer wall was demolished and the building was used to house the collection of Dr John Kirk. It opened as a museum in 1938 and in 1957 it was extended into the Debtors' Prison. Today The Castle Museum is one of the most famous Museums in Britain.

The Bar Convent

The Bar Convent was founded in 1686 when a small house and garden just outside Micklegate Bar was purchased to house a convent. In 1699, although it was illegal, the Nuns opened a boarding school for "young ladies of Roman Catholic families".

The convent and school was fully rebuilt by the architect Thomas Atkinson between 1767-1790 when the clock, made by Thomas Hindley, was installed. Today the building houses The Museum of Church History.

The Judges' Lodgings

Built in 1720 on the site of St Wilfred's church, this house was originally occupied by a well known York physician, Dr Clifton Wintringham, son of the physician to George III. Now a hotel, the building was used between 1806-1979, as its name suggests, as a lodging house for travelling Judges of Assize.

The Mansion House

When it was completed in 1730 The Mansion House was the first of its kind to be built in Britain, London's more famous counterpart being created some fifteen years later.

It is the official residence of the Lord Mayor of York, and houses the City's historic insignia, regalia and a valuable collection of silver plate.

NINTEENTH CENTURY YORK

The first half of the 19th century saw a downturn in York's fortunes. Fashions had changed and gentry no longer visited the city. The City stagnated, unemployment was high, poverty and disease were rife.

Many epidemics occurred, the worst being the cholera epidemic of 1832 which resulted in 185 deaths - one per cent of the City's population. A special burial ground outside the walls was created for the victims.

However, halfway through the century two events occurred which changed the City's fortunes.

The first was the passing of the Municipal Reform Act of 1835. This law resulted in the City forming a corporation which had the power to levy rates, and was responsible for lighting, law and order, and all water supply and sanitation.

The second event was the success of George Hudson, ex-draper and Lord Mayor of York, whose vision and entrepreneurial skills led to York becoming the centre of a new, countrywide rail network.

York's Railways

On either side of a private road linking Station Rise with Tanner Row stand two monuments to York's railway heritage.

The larger building is the headquarters building of the old North Eastern Railway, opened in 1906, and now the Headquarters of the British Rail Eastern Region.

The smaller, older building is York's first railway terminus, which opened in 1841, and was reached through a specially created arch in the town wall. By 1865 this terminus proved inadequate, especially for through traffic, and a new station was built outside the city walls, on the site of a Roman burial ground. When it was opened in 1878, the station was claimed to be the largest in the world, and today it is regarded as one of the finest examples of Victorian railway engineering in Britain.

The Yorkshire Museum

Founded by The Yorkshire Philosophical Society in 1827 on the original site of St Mary's Abbey, The Yorkshire Museum is housed in a neo-classical building set in ten acres of public park and gardens. The building was designed by William Wilkins, the architect who created the National Gallery.

In addition to housing a large collection of geological and natural history finds from all over Yorkshire, there are also galleries featuring Roman, Anglo Saxon and Viking life. Downstairs the Museum houses a collection of medieval sculpture and the remains of St Mary's Abbey.

York Art Gallery

The York Art Gallery was built in 1879 and is home for a fine collection of paintings that range from a 14th century altarpiece to works of 20th century artists such as Lowry and Paul Nash. An entire room is devoted to the work of the York artist, founder of York Art College, and saviour of the town walls, William Etty, whose statue was erected at the front of the building in 1911.

St Leonard's Place

The elegant crescent of St Leonard's Place was built between 1833-34 whilst the De Grey Rooms, now the Tourist Information Office, were built by G T Andrews in 1841-42.

Ouse Bridge    **Lendal Bridge**    **Skeldergate Bridge**

York's Bridges

York's oldest bridge is Ouse Bridge which dates back to pre Roman times. A wooden bridge collapsed on this site in 1154 and by 1435 its medieval replacement held 52 shops and tenements. The council chamber was at the north end whilst the Sheriff and Mayor had prisons built at both ends. The present structure was opened in 1820.

A ferry existed for many years at the point where Lendal Bridge crosses the river. It was replaced with a bridge to carry traffic to the newly opened station buildings. Construction began in 1860 but after a year it collapsed, killing five people. The present structure was designed by the creator of Westminster Bridge, Thomas Page, and completed in 1863.

Skeldergate Bridge was opened in 1881, also on the site of an existing ferry crossing. The small building on it was a toll house, which until 1914 collected a halfpenny fee for the crossing.

Skeldergate Bridge

Ouse Bridge

Fossgate Bridge

69

The Post Office - Lendal

York Institute - Clifford Street

Clifford Street

Clifford Street

Scattered throughout York are some fine examples of Victorian architecture, as well as reminders of the dark Victorian alleys. However Clifford Street, which houses the Fire Station, The Law Courts and The Police Station, is York's only entire Victorian Street.

Yorkshire Insurance Building

One of York's finest Victorian buildings stands in St Helen's Square, looking down Coney Street. It originally housed offices of The Yorkshire Insurance Company, and was built in 1847 by G T Andrews.

The Electric Cinema

The remains of one of York's earliest cinemas can still be seen in Fossgate. Today its elaborate archway forms the entrance to a furniture shop.

TWENTIETH CENTURY YORK

Today York is a modern, living city. Its streets are filled with a mixture of tourists and townspeople going about their daily lives. It is a thriving commercial, musical and artistic centre. Buskers and street entertainers liven up its day time pavements whilst visitors flock to its many museums and attractions.

During the post war years many new buildings and developments have occurred inside the walled city. Most of them merge successfully into their historic surroundings. Others, such as Stonebow House, arguably York's most reviled modern building, stand out as grave planning errors, and serve their purpose to remind the town planners of the future not to make the same mistakes again.

The National Railway Museum

The National Railway Museum dates back to 1927 when The London & North Eastern Railway opened Britain's first railway museum in Queen's Street.

After nationalisation a Museum of Transport opened at Clapham, and took over the running of the York museum. However, British Railways did not want to run museums, and so responsibility passed on to the Science Museum who planned the creation of a National Railway Museum. After great debate it was agreed to locate this museum in York, and in 1975 the new National Railway Museum opened to a waiting public.

The University

York University is situated outside York at Heslington. The campus first opened to students in 1963 and features some outstanding examples of modern architecture. However the oldest building on the campus is Heslington Hall, an Elizabethan Mansion built in 1568.

General Accident Building

Forsselius Garage

Stonebow

Busker - King's Square

Band - St Helen's Square

Pavement Artist

Riverside Developments

The Barbican Centre

Parliament Street

Lendal Bridge

King's Staithe

The Art's Centre

79

Technical Information

The idea for this book was born when I created the audio-visual programme "The York Story" in 1988. It has taken six years to come to fruition. The day I started the photography my Nikon F-401s gave up the ghost and died so I used a Nikkormat EL camera with a standard 50mm lens, which I picked up second hand about 15 years ago. The film stock was Kodak TMX-135. The photographs were printed by KL Photographic Laboratories York. The paper is Sequel Art 130gm supplied by Robert Horne, the typesetting and artwork by Duncan Greaves Associates, the repro was created by Reprotech Studios and the book was printed by Gareth at Itsokayco Printing - York.